Enough Already
God's Word is Sufficient

Harry L. Reeder III
(with Dave Swavely)

Editor's note by Dave Swavely: Harry and I worked on this together shortly before he went to be with the Lord, so it was his last completed writing. It was originally published in an anthology called *Whole Counsel: The Public and Private Ministries of the Word* and is used by permission.

Introduction — Why This Book?

So many people, even Christians — even well-meaning Christians — rely on something other than the Scriptures for the solutions to their spiritual problems, that sometimes I feel like crying out, "Enough already! The Bible is sufficient." We are always looking for some kind of political, psychological, sociological, philosophical, statistical, or medical insight to give us a new source of help and encouragement, when we have *enough already* in the Word of God. What we really need is to go "further up and further in" to a greater and deeper understanding of the sufficient revelation graciously granted to us by the Father, the Son, and the Holy Spirit.

One of the most important passages in the Bible is actually *about* the Bible, because it tells us where all saving and sanctifying knowledge of God is found. Second Timothy 3:16–17 says, "All Scripture is breathed out by God and profitable for teaching, for reproof, for correction, and for training in righteousness, that the man of God may be complete, equipped for every good work." That passage will provide a general framework for this discussion, though we will travel to other places in Scripture — and even in history—along the way. I want to issue a "prophetic call" for a return to this key doctrine of the faith, but I will also provide answers—some of which may be new to you—for the most commonly asked questions about it. You'll learn exactly what the doctrine of sufficiency claims about the Bible, and what it does not. We'll discuss some potential areas of misunderstanding, and I'll be very careful with my words because I know that even well-intentioned proponents of this doctrine can mislead people by their manner of presentation or imprecise language.

1

The Word is Sufficient for All Ages

Another of the most important passages in the Bible is also about the Word of God. In John 17:17 Jesus says, "Sanctify them in the truth; your word is truth." It's not that the Bible contains truth or becomes truth, but the Bible *is* the truth.

Do you realize that you own the grandest library in the history of mankind, and you can actually carry it with you wherever you go? Some of you have it in the form of paper pages, others have it on a phone or tablet, but you have a library of 66 priceless books that were written over 1600 years by 40 plus human authors guided by the Divine hand of God to record exactly what He wanted to say to us. And they are not only "Scriptures," but they are "the Scripture"—a singular collection where all the parts communicate the same themes and never contradict one another. They don't just contain truths—they are *the truth* in which the triune God of glory reveals the preeminence of Jesus Christ as our Creator, Redeemer, and Sustainer. The Word contains the timeless message of not only who made you but how He saves you—

how you can be assured you're right with Him and know where you're headed for all eternity. It's a message you desperately need to hear because of the warning, also contained in the Scriptures, that if you don't have this Savior, you're headed for eternal condemnation in a terrible place called hell.

How do we know all these things? Because the Bible tells us so. That's why I say that 2 Timothy 3:16-17 is such a crucial text in the Bible. There are many other great verses that say amazing things like God loved the world and gave His only Son and there is no condemnation for us in Christ Jesus, but we first have to trust the Scriptures to believe those things are true. Some passages tell us who made us and how to find purpose for our lives, but there are other religious books that talk about those topics. We as Christians, however, are "People of the Book" who receive the Bible as the only true Word of God to man.

The Bible clearly and repeatedly claims that it came from God. It's not man's word about God but God's Word to man. That's why everything in it is true, because it came from God and God cannot lie. It's the only way we could have a collection of books written over 1600 years with a singular message that is infallible, inerrant, reliable, and unbreakable. God is the Divine Author, revealing Himself through the human authors. Those authors did not robotically record words that were mystically dictated to them—they wrote out of their own conscious thoughts and experiences. But God had prepared them ahead of time—who their parents were, what their DNA was, where they were from, what they were going to address, the circumstances of their childhood, the content of their education—and then guided them to write all that was according to His will. He wanted to bridge the gap between God and man and give us a kind of verbal revelation that we could understand, so He communicated the Scriptures through human beings. The Holy Spirit carried along prophets and apostles to provide for us a Word of God that is both comprehendible and dependable (2 Pet. 1:19-21).

Since the Bible is "breathed out by God," as Paul says, that means it's also "profitable for teaching, for reproof, for correction, and for training in righteousness." All Scripture is profitable, or—as another translation says—"useful." It's not useful because it's a holy book that emanates vibrations as it sits on a coffee table. It's useful when you use it. God has given you the Bible to use so that God will use you when you live out the Bible by His Holy Spirit. And the proper use of the Bible starts with hearing the preaching of the Word and then studying it for yourself.

The Berean Christians are commended in Acts 17:11 because "they received the word with all eagerness, examining the Scriptures daily to see if these things were so." They had prioritized the preaching of the Word of God in their lives and were teachable when hearing it, but they weren't so open-minded that their brains were falling out. They examined the Scriptures daily for themselves. Likewise, you should "do your best to present yourself to God as one approved, a worker who has no need to be ashamed, rightly handling the word of truth" (2 Tim. 2:15). Realize that Jesus Himself is speaking to you when you hear and study the Bible, and that you are walking in His presence when you obey it and apply it to your life. "My sheep hear my voice, and I know them, and they follow me," He says in John 10:27. "Faith comes from hearing, and hearing through the word of Christ" (Rom. 10:17).

So what is the Bible useful for? It is useful to transform your life. First of all, it teaches you: "All Scripture is inspired by God and is profitable for teaching." Your behavior reveals what you believe, and what you believe affects your behavior, so the Bible tells us what to believe about God and all He has done for us. Then it is useful for "reproof"—it tells you where you are wrong in your beliefs and behavior, because like all of us you're a sinner who needs "to put off your old self, which belongs to your former manner of life and is corrupt through deceitful desires" (Eph. 4:22). Then the Bible provides "correction" and "training in righteousness," because you also need "to be renewed in the spirit of your minds, and to put on the new self, created after the likeness of God in true righteousness and holiness" (Eph. 4:23-24).

The righteousness spoken of in those passages is not the kind that earns your standing in heaven. What makes you right with God is the perfect righteousness of Christ given to you as a free gift through faith in Him. But this is a practical righteousness that reveals your desire to become more and more like your Savior on your way to heaven. "If anyone is in Christ, he is a new creation. The old has passed away; behold, the new has come. All this is from God, who through Christ reconciled us to himself" (2 Cor. 5:17-18). All Scripture is breathed out by God and profitable for this new life in Christ, for growing you in His grace and growing you by

His grace, as the Holy Spirit fills you and the Word of Christ dwells richly within you (Eph. 5:18, Col. 3:16).

These dynamics are all as true today as they were when the Bible was written. God didn't go to all the trouble of producing over a thousand pages of revelation for ancient believers just to leave subsequent generations to fend for ourselves, with only the changing winds of human knowledge and culture to rely on. No, as He told both Israel and the early church, "The grass withers, and the flower falls, but *the word of the Lord remains forever*. And this word is the good news that was preached to you" (Isa. 40:7-8, 1 Pet. 2:24-25).

Contrary to a common conception today, the findings of modern science, medicine, and psychology—though often helpful in various ways—are not *necessary* in order to solve problems that the Bible calls "sin" (disobedience to God's commands) or to live a life that is pleasing to God and blessed for us. If we did need more than the truths of the Word applied in our lives, then that would mean millions of believers who lived prior to the modern age were unable to obey God in important areas of their lives, and verses like 2 Timothy 3:16-17 would be meaningless. So would 1 Corinthians 10:13, which says, "No temptation has overtaken you but such as is common to man; and God is faithful, who will not allow you to be tempted beyond what you are able, but with the temptation will provide the way of escape also, that you may be able to endure it."

2

The Word is Sufficient for
Our Spiritual Needs

Second Timothy 3:16–17 says, "All Scripture is breathed out by God and profitable...*that the man of God may be complete, equipped for every good work.*" This last part of the passage speaks most directly to the sufficiency of Scripture. Paul says that through the Word we can be "complete," which could also be translated "adequate" or "fully qualified." We don't need the Bible plus other sources of revelation or information to be "complete, equipped for every good work"— that is Paul's main point in verse 17. But his words there also help us to understand exactly what the Bible is sufficient for, and what it is not.

The Scope of Sufficiency
"Every good work" is what the Scriptures enable us to perform, and such good works are defined in the context of 2 Timothy 3:16-17, as well as in the rest of the New Testament. To start with the immediate context, notice the verse right before: "From childhood you have been acquainted with the sacred writings, which are

able to make you wise for salvation through faith in Christ Jesus" (v. 15). Paul is speaking about *spiritual works* related to salvation and growth in Christ—not that we are saved by our works, of course, but that our obedience and service for the Lord is a fruit and evidence of our salvation, as Ephesians 2:8-10 makes clear:

> By grace you have been saved through faith. And this is not your own doing; it is the gift of God, not a result of works, so that no one may boast. For we are his workmanship, created in Christ Jesus for good works, which God pre- pared beforehand, that we should walk in them.

My works are not the basis of my salvation and acceptance before God, lest I would have something to boast about. But I always tell people to keep reading after verse 9. He who has done the work to save us is working on us and in us. On the way to the cross I don't bring any works to offer to God—"nothing in my hands I bring, simply to the cross I cling." But because of my gratefulness for the cross, I pray, "Oh God, help me to do good works for my Savior."

The verses immediately following, in 2 Tim- othy 4:1-5, also help us to understand what "every good work" means:

I charge you in the presence of God and of Christ Jesus, who is to judge the living and the dead, and by his appearing and his kingdom: preach the word; be ready in season and out of season; reprove, rebuke, and exhort, with complete patience and teaching. For the time is coming when people will not endure sound teaching, but having itching ears they will accumulate for themselves teachers to suit their own passions, and will turn away from listening to the truth and wander off into myths. As for you, always be sober-minded, endure suffering, do the work of an evangelist, fulfill your ministry.

So when Paul says the Scriptures are sufficient for "every good work," he means they are enough for our *spiritual needs* of salvation, sanctification, and service for the Lord. How should I worship God, for example? According to the Word, I should "worship in spirit and truth" (John 4:24). Where do I find out what it means to worship in truth? "Your Word is truth," Jesus says, so we go to the Bible for the answer. How can I be a witness for Christ? He tells us in the Word why we should be witnesses for Him, how to be a witness, and what happens when we witness. The Word tells us many important things about evangelism like how we are free from the pressure of having to convert someone, because that is God's job, though He will use us to plant and water the seed. It is "only God who gives the growth" (2 Cor. 3:5-9).

If you want to know how to be a godly husband or wife or father or mother, go to God's Word. What does it mean to be a servant leader? What does it mean to lay down my life for others? How do you parent? You learn all this from God's Word. I want Jesus to use me in my children's lives. I want to raise them up in the nurture and admonition of the Lord. The Lord tells you how to do this. The Lord tells you how to be a Christian employer and a Christian employee, how to be in the world but not of the world, and how to be liberated from the love of money and be a good steward. I could go on citing examples, but suffice to say (no pun intended) that God's Word is sufficient for "every good work." Everything I need to know to serve Christ in a way that honors Him is in the Bible, either explicitly or implicitly.

"The sufficiency of Scripture" does not mean that the Bible speaks directly to every single issue human beings face, of course, but that it tells us everything we *need* to know in order to live a life that pleases God (Psa. 19:7-11, 2 Pet. 1:3). The Bible does not tell us whether to go to a chiropractor or an M.D. for a back problem, for example (though we can gain wisdom from the Word that may help us in the choice). But the Bible does tell us how we can think and act in a godly way even if our back problems worsen. Though it would be nice, we don't have to be free from physical discomfort to please the Lord (cf. 2 Cor. 12:7-10), so the details of medical science are not *necessary* for us to know and therefore are not included in God's sufficient revelation. We thank God, of course, for medical and other scientific advancements in the modern world, but we should not place our trust in sources other than the Word for the answers to the spiritual issues we face.

Someone might say, "You've been talking about physical and spiritual issues, but what about 'mental,' 'emotional,' and 'psychological' problems?" I have concerns about the typical use of those terms because many of the problems being described by them are spiritual in nature. As such, their causes and cures are primarily spiritual, so they are best addressed by a wise application of the principles in the Word of God. In fact, the Bible describes the state of our minds, emotions, and souls ("psychology" means "study of the soul") as spiritual dynamics that can only be truly and permanently altered through the power of the Holy Spirit (Rom. 12:2; Gal. 5:16-25).

The widespread practice of describing problems in those areas of life as "mental illnesses" or "psychological disorders" did not come from the Bible, of course, but rather from the thinking and teaching of non-Christian psychiatrists and psychologists like Sigmund Freud, William James, Carl Jung, Abraham Maslow, etc. And the philosophies and approaches in those fields vary widely from person to person and from time to time. In contrast, however, notice what Psalm 119 says about the Scriptures:

> Forever, O Lord, your word is firmly fixed in the heavens. (v. 89)

> Your commandment makes me wiser than my enemies, for it is ever with me. I have more understanding than all my teachers, for your testimonies are my meditation. I understand more than the aged, for I keep your precepts. (vv. 98-100)

> Your word is a lamp to my feet and a light to my path. (v. 105)

The importance of Scripture in the issues of life simply cannot be overstated, nor can the danger we face if we neglect it and rely on "broken cisterns that can hold no water" (Jer. 2:13). All truth is not in the Bible, but everything in the Bible is true, and all the truth we need to know to come to Christ and follow Christ is in the Bible.

A Historic Battle for Sufficiency

About 500 years ago, on October 31, 1517, a monk named Martin Luther who was teaching at the University of Wittenberg nailed his 95 Theses to the door of the church, and the Reformation was born. What fueled Luther and the movement that followed, as much as anything, was a rediscovery of the lost doctrine of the sufficiency of Scripture.

What was the world like back then? Europe was full of tyrants—a thin layer of political and religious aristocrats who controlled everything and struck fear in the hearts of any who would oppose them. The streets of the cities were filled with physical and moral filth—trash and sewage as well as all kinds of promiscuity and perversion displayed openly. If you were to go into a church back then you wouldn't have participated in the worship—you would have merely watched and listened, and nothing you heard would have been in your own language. There would have been no hymn book and no congregational singing. Monks might engage in chanting but even that would be in Latin, a language you wouldn't understand.

Worst of all, the church you attend would have been part of a religious movement that had long forgotten the biblical Gospel that spread into Europe a thousand years earlier and transformed millions of lives, setting them free from paganism and creating vital Christian communities and cultures. That spiritual freedom was now just a mere dream of the past—in its place were empty rituals, superstitions, religious manipulation, and a system of works salvation that offered the possibility of Divine acceptance only if you put enough effort into the sacraments of the church. If you attended mass faithfully, confessed your sins to the priest, and did all the acts of penance as prescribed by him, you might make it to heaven after a long time in purgatory. The people of Europe were in bondage once again to a pagan religion, though now it went by the name "Christian." And of course there was not only moral corruption in the world, but also in the church, because the world had made its way into the church so much that the two were hardly distinguishable.

Martin Luther could take no more when he saw John Tetzel going from town to town selling indulgences so people could buy themselves and their loved ones into heaven. Tetzel would say something like, "As soon as the coin in the coffer rings, a soul from purgatory springs." Luther wrote his 95 Theses in response to that kind of false religion and then went on to publish many more books about the Gospel, sparking the movement we call the Reformation, which in later generations spawned a missionary movement that reached the ends of the earth with the truth about Christ.

Central to the faith and ministry of Luther and the other Reformers were five "solas"—*sola Scriptura, sola fide, sola gratia, solus Christus,* and *soli deo gloria. Sola Scriptura,* which means "Scripture alone" in Latin, is usually listed first because it's foundational to the rest. And the word "alone" was key in distinguishing true biblical doctrine from the falsehoods of the medieval church. People would say that they were saved by faith or by grace, for example, but they would never say "by faith alone" or "by grace alone." Likewise, they would say they believed the Bible but they wouldn't say the Bible was the only source of Divine revelation. They believed that the church and its councils (i.e. the interpretations and additions of men) were of equal authority to the Scriptures in spiritual matters and therefore were necessary for people to know God.

But you can't add to the Scripture without taking away its power, "thus making void the word of God by your tradition that you have handed down," as Jesus said in Mark 7:13.

Luther, in his commentary on Romans, agrees:

> If you now attempt, in this spiritual conflict, to protect yourself by the help of man without the Word of God, you simply enter upon the conflict with that mighty spirit, the devil, naked and unprotected. Such an endeavor would be worse than David against Goliath—without God's supernatural power helping David. You may, therefore, if you so please, oppose your power to the might of the devil. It will then be very easily seen what an utterly unequal conflict it is, if one does not have at hand in the beginning the Word of God.

3

The Word is Sufficient for
our Spiritual Warfare

Will you rely on the Scriptures for your spiritual help and hope, as Martin Luther encouraged and exemplified? You will hear that we are in a "culture war," but the fact is we are in a *spiritual* war where the culture is a battlefield for the souls of men and women and the fate of the nations that comprise them. This war didn't start anytime recently—it's been going on since the dawn of time. There was a war on Jesus and His truth in the 15th Century and long before that in the First Century, when believers first took the Gospel to the world. At that time there was a state power that said you can have your Christianity as long as you also bow to Caesar. The early Christians said, "No. We will respect Caesar, but Caesar is not Lord—only Jesus is Lord." And many of them paid the price of martyrdom for their faith.

The war started all the way back in the Garden, when Satan said to Eve, "Did God actually say…?" He questioned whether God's Word was true, and then he attacked its sufficiency by suggesting that Adam and Eve needed the "knowledge of good and evil" in addition to what God had already told them. And Satan has continued to press these same attacks upon us, in different forms, right up until today. But know this: the war has already been won. Jesus Christ died to win it, and the grave could not hold Him—He rose victorious over all the enemies of God and His people. He has not yet destroyed them utterly—He'll do that when He comes back—but be assured that He has defeated them. So we do not fear. We do not live in anxiety. We certainly have many difficulties and concerns living in a sin-cursed world, but we live with a confidence from the Word of God that Jesus Christ is the Savior of sinners.

I'm a sinner and I need a Savior. Jesus Christ has won the victory for me. He has ascended and is now interceding for His people. He will come again and not one of His will be lost. This Kingdom Gospel will continue to go from nation to nation and people will be saved "from every tribe and language and people and nation" (Rev. 5:9). That's what I know. Why? Because the Bible tells me so.

So we are in the same war that has been going on throughout history, and we are on this side of the cross. Jesus already won the war in the sense of assuring ultimate victory and releasing all the nations from the grip of Satan, but now we're fighting the mop-up battles as we go from nation to nation, neighborhood to neighborhood, and family to family, unleashing the truth of the Gospel with the weapons of the Spirit. On the one hand we stand firm on the truth of God's Word and then on the other hand we move forward to take every thought captive to the obedience of Christ. We go forward with evangelism and discipleship and we ask God to allow us to be a light for Him in this world. And as we do, His Word is the lamp to our feet and the light to our path.

It is by this Word that I understand everything in life. How He made me. How He saved me and where I'm headed for in the next life. The Bible tells me all of this. There is a war; Satan is raging. He has not been totally debilitated but he has been defeated. So his rage we can endure. One little word shall fell him. We do not run from him but we enter the fray with humility, compassion, graciousness, confidence, and courage to bring the truth into this world.

That is what our forbearers did when the U.S. Supreme Court made horrendous decisions like declaring that a slave was only 3/5 of a person. Those who knew the Word of God said that was the height of stupidity, determining to expose the error and preach the truth in love. It took William Wilberforce 48 years in England to convince an entire nation that man-stealing was wrong. He didn't resign himself to the unjust laws and magisterial dictates of his culture but fought against them in the name of Christ.

Many of us were shocked and appalled in 1973 when our Supreme Court decided that unborn children were no longer persons with a right to life. On the basis of God's Word, we began to proclaim the sacredness of life, the call to mercy and grace for those who are in crisis pregnancies, and the need for opening our homes for adoption. The same thing has happened recently regarding our nation's marriage laws. The Supreme Court can say all they want to about marriage, but the fact is that God Himself designed it to be a sacred reflection of Christ's relationship with His people and established it as one man and one woman for life. Sexual intimacy was designed to be enjoyed only as a part of such biblical marriages. All believers should embrace that truth personally and proclaim it graciously but confidently. We also know from God's Word that our identity is not to be found in our sexual proclivities or practices. My identity is that I was made in the image of God, and by God's grace I can be restored to that image in Jesus Christ, who now becomes my identity as Lord and Savior, freeing me from sin's guilt and power.

Those are just some examples of the many spiritual battles we face in our culture, in addition to the constant conflicts with the world, the flesh, and the devil in our own personal lives. But whatever kinds of warfare we face, our most effective weapon is always "the sword of the Spirit, which is the Word of God" (Eph. 6:17). So we must know the Word of God. The Word of God must shape everything about what we believe and how we behave. It is our guide in every essential area of life. That would be my number one thesis if I were to put together a list like Martin Luther did. And I hope I will have the same commitment and courage he showed when his life was on the line in front of the political and religious powers of his day. He said to them,

> Since your majesty and your lordships desire a simple reply, I will answer without horns and without teeth. Unless I am convicted by Scripture and plain reason—I do not accept the authority of popes and councils for they have contradicted each other—my conscience is captive to the Word of God. I cannot and I will not

recant anything, for to go against conscience is neither right nor safe. Here I stand, I cannot do otherwise, God help me. Amen.

By God's providence, Martin Luther's life was spared that day, and he went on to serve the Lord for 25 more years. His faith in the sufficiency of Scripture never diminished, and shortly before his death he wrote this poem:

> Feelings come and feelings go,
> And feelings are deceiving;
> My warrant is the Word of God—
> Naught else is worth believing.
> Though all my heart should feel condemned
> For want of some sweet token,
> There is One greater than my heart
> Whose Word cannot be broken.
> I'll trust in God's unchanging Word
> Till soul and body sever,
> For, though all things shall pass away,
> HIS WORD SHALL STAND FOREVER!

My primary concern in our spiritual warfare today is not the wolves howling at the door of the culture at large, but the termites eating at the floor of the professing church of Jesus Christ. It is the center that must hold.

Every time I stand in my pulpit, I'm reminded of the Bible that was buried under it when the church was built. I remember that our founding pastor, when I succeeded him, handed me a Bible and said, "I don't know what a mantle is, but this is yours. Preach it!"

I love the Word of God because without it I wouldn't know the God of the Word. I wouldn't know that He loved me or saved me or how to deal with any of the most important issues of life. I can't believe I've had the privilege of preaching this incomparable book for almost 50 blessed years.

What I preach for and pray for is that God's people will love God's Word and it will shape us all more and more into the image of His Son Jesus Christ, by the power of the Holy Spirit. And I believe God's Word is sufficient for every good work.

When I was six years old and first learned "The B-I-B-L-E," I had no idea how much theology is in that little song. It's so deep that it even has a double meaning: "The B-I-B-L-E, yes that's the book for me. I stand alone on the Word of God..." We stand alone on the Bible in the sense of *sola Scriptura* — it is the only authoritative Word of God, sufficient for all ages, for all our spiritual needs, and for all our spiritual battles. But also, "I stand alone" means that even if no one else stands with me in the fight for the authority and sufficiency of Scripture, I will still remain faithful to those doctrines because what I'm really doing is standing in Christ, the One who said, "Your Word is truth."

It *is* the truth, and it will set you free.

About the Authors

Harry L. Reeder, III (BA Covenant College, MDiv Westminster Theological Seminary, DMin Reformed Theological Seminary) pastored Pinelands Presbyterian Church in Miami, FL; Christ Covenant Church in Charlotte, NC; and Briarwood Presbyterian Church in Birmingham, AL.

Harry is the author of numerous theological articles and has written chapters for various volumes. He is the author of *From Embers to a Flame: How God Can*

Revitalize Your Church, *3D Leadership*, and a commentary on James in the *Lectio Continua* series. He hosted *Today in Perspective*, a daily podcast on current events from a Biblical worldview with Gospel solutions, as well as *Fresh Bread*, a daily devotional podcast.

Harry was adjunct faculty at Birmingham Theological Seminary, Reformed Theological Seminary, and Westminster Theological Seminary (where he was a Board member for more than 30 years).

About the Authors

Dave Swavely (MDiv The Master's Seminary) is President of the nonprofit ministry The Way With Words. He is the author of many books, both non-fiction and fiction, and has edited and published many more by other authors.

Dave and his wife Jill have been married for over 30 years, with seven children and five grandchildren. Together they've started three churches and two schools and housed many people in need. He was a personal assistant to the world-renowned speaker and author Dr. John MacArthur in the 1990s and has spoken at various conferences around the country and abroad.

Dave's life journey has included many failures as well as successes, and he's learned the most from his failures.

Also Published by The Way With Words

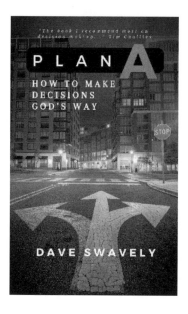

God has a wonderful plan for your life (specifically for your decision making)! We make choices, and then our choices make us (or break us!). This is true of "big" decisions, of course—the ones we agonize over as we approach them, and often regret horribly after we have made them. But the "little" decisions are just as important, because they lead to the big ones. Dave Swavely has spent a long lifetime studying what the Bible says about God's leading, helping others to apply those principles, and making decisions himself (and learning even more from the bad ones). In this short but profound book, he presents an easy-to-follow "Plan A" that will always lead to the best decisions you can make—because they are based on God's Word and wisdom.

Also Published by The Way With Words

Have you ever wondered what actually happens in biblical counseling? Do you want to learn more about important issues like abuse, submission, and self-image? Is your own spiritual life or marriage in need of hope and help? Lori Beard is an ACBC certified counselor and Alison Simmons was her counselee. Based on their journals, this book is case study recounting the challenges and blessings of a biblical counseling process from beginning to end. This unique book is helpful for use in counseling training, for encouraging people to consider entering the process, and for dispelling common misunderstandings of a biblical approach to helping people. The book is instructive, motivational, and enjoyable for anyone who likes a captivating real-life story.

Also Published by The Way With Words

What if...?

This "fly on the wall" story imagines that Spurgeon made a clandestine visit to Dickens' home when the author was nearing death. The epic conversation between these two great wordsmiths not only entertains but also elevates our understanding of important life and death issues.

Also Published by The Way With Words

Can't hear. Can't see. Can't move. Can't breathe.
What do you do when all you are met with in life is "can't"? Every day people experience seemingly insurmountable obstacles. But how can you persevere when the cause of your struggle is a total mystery? *Paige's Pages* is the inspiring story of a young woman who has spent most of her life battling an undiagnosed disease that has threatened to take her life countless times. This book takes you on a rollercoaster ride of joy and pain alongside a family searching for an answer. When Paige is on the brink of giving up, God grants grace and hope to keep going. *Paige's Pages* is a heart-warming reminder that sometimes the answer to prayer is not an end to the pain and struggle, but joy in the midst of suffering.

Made in the USA
Middletown, DE
01 August 2024

58338724R00024